# THE METAPHYSICAL ELEMENTS OF ETHICS

## By

## Immanuel Kant

# INTRODUCTION TO THE METAPHYSICAL ELEMENTS OF ETHICS

Ethics in ancient times signified moral philosophy (philosophia moralis) generally, which was also called the doctrine of duties. Subsequently it was found advisable to confine this name to a part of moral philosophy, namely, to the doctrine of duties which are not subject to external laws (for which in German the name Tugendlehre was found suitable). Thus the system of general deontology is divided into that of jurisprudence (jurisprudentia), which is capable of external laws, and of ethics, which is not thus capable, and we may let this division stand.

## I. Exposition of the Conception of Ethics

The notion of duty is in itself already the notion of a constraint of the free elective will by the law; whether this constraint be an external one or be self-constraint. The moral imperative, by its categorical (the unconditional ought) announces this constraint, which therefore does not apply to all rational beings (for there may also be holy beings), but applies to men as rational physical beings who are unholy enough to be seduced by pleasure to the transgression of the moral law, although they themselves recognize its authority; and when they do obey it, to obey it unwillingly (with resistance of their inclination); and it is in this that the constraint properly consists. Now, as man is a free (moral) being, the notion of duty can contain only self-constraint (by the idea of the law itself), when we look to the internal determination of the will (the spring), for thus only is it possible to combine that constraint (even if it were external) with the freedom of the elective will. The notion of duty then must be an ethical one.

The impulses of nature, then, contain hindrances to the fulfilment of duty in the mind of man, and resisting forces, some of them powerful; and he must judge himself able to combat these and to conquer them by means of reason, not in the future, but in the present, simultaneously with the thought; he must judge that he can do what the law unconditionally commands that he ought.

Now the power and resolved purpose to resist a strong but unjust opponent is called fortitude (fortitudo), and when concerned with the opponent of the moral character within us, it is virtue (virtus, fortitudo moralis). Accordingly, general deontology, in that part which brings not external, but internal, freedom under laws is the doctrine of virtue.

Jurisprudence had to do only with the formal condition of external freedom (the condition of consistency with itself, if its maxim became a universal law), that is, with law. Ethics, on the contrary, supplies us with a matter (an object of the free elective will), an end of pure reason which is at the same time conceived as an objectively necessary end, i.e., as duty for all men. For, as the sensible inclinations mislead us to ends (which are the matter of the elective will) that may contradict duty, the legislating reason cannot otherwise guard against their influence than by an opposite moral end, which therefore must be given a priori independently on inclination.

An end is an object of the elective will (of a rational being) by the idea of which this will is determined to an action for the production of this object. Now I may be forced by others to actions which are directed to an end as means, but I cannot be forced to have an end; I can only make something an end to myself. If, however, I am also bound to make something which lies in the notions of practical reason an end to myself, and therefore besides the formal determining principle of the elective will (as contained in law) to have also a material principle, an end which can be opposed to the end derived from sensible impulses; then this gives the notion of an end which is in itself a duty. The doctrine of this cannot belong to jurisprudence, but to ethics, since this alone includes in its conception self-constraint according to moral laws.

For this reason, ethics may also be defined as the system of the ends of the pure practical reason. The two parts of moral philosophy are distinguished as treating respectively of ends and of duties of constraint. That ethics contains duties to the observance of which one cannot be (physically) forced by others, is merely the consequence of this, that it is a doctrine of ends, since to be forced to have ends or to set them before one's self is a contradiction.

Now that ethics is a doctrine of virtue (doctrina officiorum virtutis) follows from the definition of virtue given above compared with the obligation, the peculiarity of which has just been shown. There is in fact no other determination of the elective will, except that to an end, which in the very notion of it implies that I cannot even physically be forced to it by the elective will of others. Another may indeed force me to do something which is not my end (but only means to the end of another), but he cannot force me to make it my own end, and yet I can have no end except of my own making. The latter supposition would be a contradiction- an act of freedom which yet at the same time would not be free. But there is no contradiction in setting before one's self an end which is also a duty: for in this case I constrain myself, and this is quite consistent with freedom. But how is such an end possible? That is now the question. For the possibility of the notion of the thing (viz., that it is not self-contradictory) is not enough to prove the possibility of the thing itself (the objective reality of the notion).

## II. Exposition of the Notion of an End which is also a Duty

We can conceive the relation of end to duty in two ways; either starting from the end to find the maxim of the dutiful actions; or conversely, setting out from this to find the end which is also duty. Jurisprudence proceeds in the former way. It is left to everyone's free elective will what end he will choose for his action. But its maxim is determined a priori; namely, that the freedom of the agent must be consistent with the freedom of every other according to a universal law.

Ethics, however, proceeds in the opposite way. It cannot start from the ends which the man may propose to himself, and hence give directions as to the maxims he should adopt, that is, as to his duty; for that would be to take empirical principles of maxims, and these could not give any notion of duty; since this, the categorical ought, has its root in pure reason alone. Indeed, if the maxims were to be adopted in accordance with those ends (which are all selfish), we could not properly speak of the notion of duty at all. Hence in ethics the notion of duty must lead to ends, and must on moral principles give the foundation of maxims with respect to the ends which we ought to propose to ourselves.

Setting aside the question what sort of end that is which is in itself a duty, and how such an end is possible, it is here only necessary to show that a duty of this kind is called a duty of virtue, and why it is so called.

To every duty corresponds a right of action (facultas moralis generatim), but all duties do not imply a corresponding right (facultas juridica) of another to compel anyone, but only the duties called legal duties. Similarly to all ethical obligation corresponds the notion of virtue, but it does not follow that all ethical duties are duties of virtue. Those, in fact, are not so which do not concern so much a certain end (matter, object of the elective will), but merely that which is formal in the moral determination of the will (e.g., that the dutiful action must also be done from duty). It is only an end which is also duty that can be called a duty of virtue. Hence there are several of the latter kind (and thus there are distinct virtues); on the contrary, there is only one duty of the former kind, but it is one which is valid for all actions (only one virtuous disposition).

The duty of virtue is essentially distinguished from the duty of justice in this respect; that it is morally possible to be externally compelled to the latter, whereas the former rests on free self-constraint only. For finite holy beings (which cannot even be tempted to the violation of duty) there is no doctrine of virtue, but only moral philosophy, the latter being an autonomy of practical reason, whereas the former is also an autocracy of it. That is, it includes a consciousness- not indeed immediately perceived, but rightly concluded, from the moral categorical imperative- of the power to become master of one's inclinations which resist the law; so that human morality in its highest stage can yet be nothing more than virtue; even if it were quite pure (perfectly free from the influence of a spring foreign to duty), a state which is poetically personified under the name of the wise man (as an ideal to which one should continually approximate).

Virtue, however, is not to be defined and esteemed merely as habit, and (as it is expressed in the prize essay of Cochius) as a long custom acquired by practice of morally good actions. For, if this is not an effect of well-resolved and firm principles ever more and more purified, then, like any other mechanical arrangement brought about by technical practical reason, it is neither armed for all circumstances nor adequately secured against the change that may be wrought by new allurements.

## REMARK

To virtue = + a is opposed as its logical contradictory (contradictorie oppositum) the negative lack of virtue (moral weakness) = 0; but vice = - a is its contrary (contrarie s. realiter oppositum); and it is not merely a needless question but an offensive one to ask whether great crimes do not perhaps demand more strength of mind than great virtues. For by strength of mind we understand the strength of purpose of a man, as a being endowed with freedom, and consequently so far as he is master of himself (in his senses) and therefore in a healthy condition of mind. But great crimes are paroxysms, the very sight of which makes the man of healthy mind shudder. The question would therefore be something like this: whether a man in a fit of madness can have more physical strength than if he is in his senses; and we may admit this without on that account ascribing to him more strength of mind, if by mind we understand the vital principle of man in the free use of his powers. For since those crimes have their ground merely in the power of the inclinations that weaken reason, which does not prove strength of mind, this question would be nearly the same as the question whether a man in a fit of illness can show more strength than in a healthy condition; and this may be directly denied, since the want of health, which consists in the proper balance of all the bodily forces of the man, is a weakness in the system of these forces, by which system alone we can estimate absolute health.

III. Of the Reason for conceiving an End which is also a Duty

An end is an object of the free elective will, the idea of which determines this will to an action by which the object is produced. Accordingly every action has its end, and as no one can have an end without himself making the object of his elective will his end, hence to have some end of actions is an act of the freedom of the agent, not an affect of physical nature. Now, since this act which determines an end is a practical principle which commands not the means (therefore not conditionally) but the end itself (therefore unconditionally), hence it is a categorical imperative of pure practical reason and one, therefore, which combines a concept of duty with that of an end in general.

Now there must be such an end and a categorical imperative corresponding to it. For since there are free actions, there must also be ends to which as an object those actions are directed. Amongst these ends there must also be some which are at the same time (that is, by their very notion) duties. For if there were none such, then since no actions can be without an end, all ends which practical reason might have would be valid only as means to other ends, and a categorical imperative would be impossible; a supposition which destroys all moral philosophy.

Here, therefore, we treat not of ends which man actually makes to himself in accordance with the sensible impulses of his nature, but of objects of the free elective will under its own laws- objects which he ought to make his end. We may call the former technical (subjective), properly pragmatical, including the rules of prudence in the choice of its ends; but the latter we must call the moral (objective) doctrine of ends. This distinction is, however, superfluous here, since moral philosophy already by its very notion is clearly separated from the doctrine of physical nature (in the present instance, anthropology). The latter resting on empirical principles, whereas the moral doctrine of ends which treats of duties rests on principles given a priori in pure practical reason.

### IV. What are the Ends which are also Duties?

They are: A. OUR OWN PERFECTION, B. HAPPINESS OF OTHERS.

We cannot invert these and make on one side our own happiness, and on the other the perfection of others, ends which should be in themselves duties for the same person.

For one's own happiness is, no doubt, an end that all men have (by virtue of the impulse of their nature), but this end cannot without contradiction be regarded as a duty. What a man of himself inevitably wills does not come under the notion of duty, for this is a constraint to an end reluctantly adopted. It is, therefore, a contradiction to say that a man is in duty bound to advance his own happiness with all his power.

It is likewise a contradiction to make the perfection of another my end, and to regard myself as in duty bound to promote it. For it is just in this that the perfection of another man as a person consists, namely, that he is able of himself to set before him his own end according to his own notions of duty; and it is a contradiction to require (to make it a duty for me) that I should do something which no other but himself can do.

## V. Explanation of these two Notions

### A. OUR OWN PERFECTION

The word perfection is liable to many misconceptions. It is sometimes understood as a notion belonging to transcendental philosophy; viz., the notion of the totality of the manifold which taken together constitutes a thing; sometimes, again, it is understood as belonging to teleology, so that it signifies the correspondence of the properties of a thing to an end. Perfection in the former sense might be called quantitative (material), in the latter qualitative (formal) perfection. The former can be one only, for the whole of what belongs to the one thing is one. But of the latter there may be several in one thing; and it is of the latter property that we here treat.

When it is said of the perfection that belongs to man generally (properly speaking, to humanity), that it is in itself a duty to make this our end, it must be placed in that which may be the effect of one's deed, not in that which is merely an endowment for which we have to thank nature; for otherwise it would not be duty. Consequently, it can be nothing else than the cultivation of one's power (or natural capacity) and also of one's will (moral disposition) to satisfy the requirement of duty in general. The supreme element in the former (the power) is the understanding, it being the faculty of concepts, and, therefore, also of those concepts which refer to duty. First it is his duty to labour to raise himself out of the rudeness of his nature, out of his animal nature more and more to humanity, by which alone he is capable of setting before him ends to supply the defects of his ignorance by instruction, and to correct his errors;

he is not merely counselled to do this by reason as technically practical, with a view to his purposes of other kinds (as art), but reason, as morally practical, absolutely commands him to do it, and makes this end his duty, in order that he may be worthy of the humanity that dwells in him. Secondly, to carry the cultivation of his will up to the purest virtuous disposition, that, namely, in which the law is also the spring of his dutiful actions, and to obey it from duty, for this is internal morally practical perfection. This is called the moral sense (as it were a special sense, sensus moralis), because it is a feeling of the effect which the legislative will within himself exercises on the faculty of acting accordingly. This is, indeed, often misused fanatically, as though (like the genius of Socrates) it preceded reason, or even could dispense with judgement of reason; but still it is a moral perfection, making every special end, which is also a duty, one's own end.

## B. HAPPINESS OF OTHERS

It is inevitable for human nature that man a should wish and seek for happiness, that is, satisfaction with his condition, with certainty of the continuance of this satisfaction. But for this very reason it is not an end that is also a duty. Some writers still make a distinction between moral and physical happiness (the former consisting in satisfaction with one's person and moral behaviour, that is, with what one does; the other in satisfaction with that which nature confers, consequently with what one enjoys as a foreign gift). Without at present censuring the misuse of the word (which even involves a contradiction), it must be observed that the feeling of the former belongs solely to the preceding head, namely, perfection. For he who is to feel himself happy in the mere consciousness of his uprightness already possesses that perfection which in the previous section was defined as that end which is also duty.

If happiness, then, is in question, which it is to be my duty to promote as my end, it must be the happiness of other men whose (permitted) end I hereby make also mine. It still remains left to themselves to decide what they shall reckon as belonging to their happiness; only that it is in my power to decline many things which they so reckon, but which I do not so regard, supposing that they have no right to demand it from me as their own. A plausible objection often advanced against the division of duties above adopted consists in setting over against that end a supposed obligation to study my own (physical) happiness, and thus making this, which is my natural and merely subjective end, my duty (and objective end). This requires to be cleared up.

Adversity, pain, and want are great temptations to transgression of one's duty; accordingly it would seem that strength, health, a competence, and welfare generally, which are opposed to that influence, may also be regarded as ends that are also duties; that is, that it is a duty to promote our own happiness not merely to make that of others our end. But in that case the end is not happiness but the morality of the agent; and happiness is only the means of removing the hindrances to morality; permitted means, since no one has a right to demand from me the sacrifice of my not immoral ends. It is not directly a duty to seek a competence for one's self; but indirectly it may be so; namely, in order to guard against poverty which is a great temptation to vice. But then it is not my happiness but my morality, to maintain which in its integrity is at once my end and my duty.

VI. Ethics does not supply Laws for Actions (which is done by

Jurisprudence), but only for the Maxims of Action

The notion of duty stands in immediate relation to a law (even though I abstract from every end which is the matter of the law); as is shown by the formal principle of duty in the categorical imperative: "Act so that the maxims of thy action might become a universal law." But in ethics this is conceived as the law of thy own will, not of will in general, which might be that of others; for in the latter case it would give rise to a judicial duty which does not belong to the domain of ethics. In ethics, maxims are regarded as those subjective laws which merely have the specific character of universal legislation, which is only a negative principle (not to contradict a law in general). How, then, can there be further a law for the maxims of actions?

It is the notion of an end which is also a duty, a notion peculiar to ethics, that alone is the foundation of a law for the maxims of actions; by making the subjective end (that which every one has)

subordinate to the objective end (that which every one ought to make his own). The imperative: "Thou shalt make this or that thy end (e. g., the happiness of others)" applies to the matter of the elective will (an object). Now since no free action is possible, without the agent having in view in it some end (as matter of his elective will), it follows that, if there is an end which is also a duty, the maxims of actions which are means to ends must contain only the condition of fitness for a possible universal legislation: on the other hand, the end which is also a duty can make it a law that we should have such a maxim, whilst for the maxim itself the possibility of agreeing with a universal legislation is sufficient.

For maxims of actions may be arbitrary, and are only limited by the condition of fitness for a universal legislation, which is the formal principle of actions. But a law abolishes the arbitrary character of actions, and is by this distinguished from recommendation (in which one only desires to know the best means to an end).

## VII. Ethical Duties are of indeterminate, Juridical Duties of strict, Obligation

This proposition is a consequence of the foregoing; for if the law can only command the maxim of the actions, not the actions themselves, this is a sign that it leaves in the observance of it a latitude (latitudo) for the elective will; that is, it cannot definitely assign how and how much we should do by the action towards the end which is also duty. But by an indeterminate duty is not meant a permission to make exceptions from the maxim of the actions, but only the permission to limit one maxim of duty by another (e. g., the general love of our neighbour by the love of parents); and this in fact enlarges the field for the practice of virtue. The more indeterminate the duty, and the more imperfect accordingly the obligation of the man to the action, and the closer he nevertheless brings this maxim of obedience thereto (in his own mind) to the strict duty (of justice), so much the more perfect is his virtuous action.

Hence it is only imperfect duties that are duties of virtue. The fulfilment of them is merit (meritum) = + a; but their transgression is not necessarily demerit (demeritum) = - a, but only moral unworth = o, unless the agent made it a principle not to conform to those duties. The strength of purpose in the former case is alone properly called virtue [Tugend] (virtus); the weakness in the latter case is not vice (vitium), but rather only lack of virtue [Untugend], a want of moral strength (defectus moralis). (As the word Tugend is derived from taugen [to be good for something], Untugend by its etymology signifies good for nothing.) Every action contrary to duty is called transgression (peccatum). Deliberate transgression which has become a principle is what properly constitutes what is called vice (vitium).

Although the conformity of actions to justice (i.e., to be an upright man) is nothing meritorious, yet the conformity of the maxim of such actions regarded as duties, that is, reverence for justice is meritorious. For by this the man makes the right of humanity or of men his own end, and thereby enlarges his notion of duty beyond that of indebtedness (officium debiti), since although another man by virtue of his rights can demand that my actions shall conform to the law, he cannot demand that the law shall also contain the spring of these actions. The same thing is true of the general ethical command, "Act dutifully from a sense of duty." To fix this disposition firmly in one's mind and to quicken it is, as in the former case, meritorious, because it goes beyond the law of duty in actions and makes the law in itself the spring.

But just for or reason, those duties also must be reckoned as of indeterminate obligation, in respect of which there exists a subjective principle which ethically rewards them; or to bring them as near as possible to the notion of a strict obligation, a principle of susceptibility of this reward according to the law of virtue; namely, a moral pleasure which goes beyond mere satisfaction with oneself (which may be merely negative), and of which it is proudly said that in this consciousness virtue is its own reward.

When this merit is a merit of the man in respect of other men of promoting their natural ends, which are recognized as such by all men (making their happiness his own), we might call it the sweet merit, the consciousness of which creates a moral enjoyment in which men are by sympathy inclined to revel; whereas the bitter merit of promoting the true welfare of other men, even though they should not recognize it as such (in the case of the unthankful and ungrateful), has commonly no such reaction, but only produces a satisfaction with one's self, although in the latter case this would be even greater.

## VIII. Exposition of the Duties of Virtue as Intermediate Duties

### OUR OWN PERFECTION as an end which is also a duty

Physical perfection; that is, cultivation of all our faculties generally for the promotion of the ends set before us by reason. That this is a duty, and therefore an end in itself, and that the effort to effect this even without regard to the advantage that it secures us, is based, not on a conditional (pragmatic), but an unconditional (moral) imperative, may be seen from the following consideration. The power of proposing to ourselves an end is the characteristic of humanity (as distinguished from the brutes). With the end of humanity in our own person is therefore combined the rational will, and consequently the duty of deserving well of humanity by culture generally, by acquiring or advancing the power to carry out all sorts of possible ends, so far as this power is to be found in man; that is, it is a duty to cultivate the crude capacities of our nature, since it is by that cultivation that the animal is raised to man, therefore it is a duty in itself.

This duty, however, is merely ethical, that is, of indeterminate obligation. No principle of reason prescribes how far one must go in this effort (in enlarging or correcting his faculty of understanding, that is, in acquisition of knowledge or technical capacity); and besides the difference in the circumstances into which men may come makes the choice of the kind of employment for which he should cultivate his talent very arbitrary. Here, therefore, there is no law of reason for actions, but only for the maxim of actions, viz.: "Cultivate thy faculties of mind and body so as to be effective for all ends that may come in thy way, uncertain which of them may become thy own."

(b) Cultivation of Morality in ourselves. The greatest moral perfection of man is to do his duty, and that from duty (that the law be not only the rule but also the spring of his actions). Now at first sight this seems to be a strict obligation, and as if the principle of duty commanded not merely the legality of every action, but also the morality, i.e., the mental disposition, with the exactness and strictness of a law; but in fact the law commands even here only the maxim of the action, namely, that we should seek the ground of obligation, not in the sensible impulses (advantage or disadvantage), but wholly in the law; so that the action itself is not commanded. For it is not possible to man to see so far into the depth of his own heart that he could ever be thoroughly certain of the purity of his moral purpose and the sincerity of his mind even in one single action, although he has no doubt about the legality of it. Nay, often the weakness which deters a man from the risk of a crime is regarded by him as virtue (which gives the notion of strength). And how many there are who may have led a long blameless life, who are only fortunate in having escaped so many temptations. How much of the element of pure morality in their mental disposition may have belonged to each deed remains hidden even from themselves.

Accordingly, this duty to estimate the worth of one's actions not merely by their legality, but also by their morality (mental disposition), is only of indeterminate obligation; the law does not command this internal action in the human mind itself, but only the maxim of the action, namely, that we should strive with all our power that for all dutiful actions the thought of duty should be of itself an adequate spring.

HAPPINESS OF OTHERS as an end which is also a duty

Physical Welfare. Benevolent wishes may be unlimited, for they do not imply doing anything. But the case is more difficult with benevolent action, especially when this is to be done, not from friendly inclination (love) to others, but from duty, at the expense of the sacrifice and mortification of many of our appetites. That this beneficence is a duty results from this: that since our self-love cannot be separated from the need to be loved by others (to obtain help from them in case of necessity), we therefore make ourselves an end for others; and this maxim can never be obligatory except by having the specific character of a universal law, and consequently by means of a will that we should also make others our ends. Hence the happiness of others is an end that is also a duty.

I am only bound then to sacrifice to others a part of my welfare without hope of recompense: because it is my duty, and it is impossible to assign definite limits how far that may go. Much depends on what would be the true want of each according to his own feelings, and it must be left to each to determine this for himself. For that one should sacrifice his own happiness, his true wants, in order to promote that of others, would be a self-contradictory maxim if made a universal law. This duty, therefore, is only indeterminate; it has a certain latitude within which one may do more or less without our being able to assign its limits definitely. The law holds only for the maxims, not for definite actions.

Moral well-being of others (salus moralis) also belongs to the happiness of others, which it is our duty to promote, but only a negative duty. The pain that a man feels from remorse of conscience, although its origin is moral, is yet in its operation physical, like grief, fear, and every other diseased condition. To take care that he should not be deservedly smitten by this inward reproach is not indeed my duty but his business; nevertheless, it is my duty to do nothing which by the nature of man might seduce him to that for which his conscience may hereafter torment him, that is, it is my duty not to give him occasion of stumbling. But there are no definite limits within which this care for the moral satisfaction of others must be kept; therefore it involves only an indeterminate obligation.

## IX. What is a Duty of Virtue?

Virtue is the strength of the man's maxim in his obedience to duty. All strength is known only by the obstacles that it can overcome; and in the case of virtue the obstacles are the natural inclinations which may come into conflict with the moral purpose; and as it is the man who himself puts these obstacles in the way of his maxims, hence virtue is not merely a self-constraint (for that might be an effort of one inclination to constrain another), but is also a constraint according to a principle of inward freedom, and therefore by the mere idea of duty, according to its formal law.

All duties involve a notion of necessitation by the law, and ethical duties involve a necessitation for which only an internal legislation is possible; juridical duties, on the other hand, one for which external legislation also is possible. Both, therefore, include the notion of constraint, either self-constraint or constraint by others. The moral power of the former is virtue, and the action springing from such a disposition (from reverence for the law) may be called a virtuous action (ethical), although the law expresses a juridical duty. For it is the doctrine of virtue that commands us to regard the rights of men as holy.

But it does not follow that everything the doing of which is virtue, is, properly speaking, a duty of virtue. The former may concern merely the form of the maxims; the latter applies to the matter of them, namely, to an end which is also conceived as duty. Now, as the ethical obligation to ends, of which there may be many, is only indeterminate, because it contains only a law for the maxim of actions, and the end is the matter (object) of elective will; hence there are many duties, differing according to the difference of lawful ends, which may be called duties of virtue (officia honestatis), just because they are subject only to free self-constraint, not to the constraint of other men, and determine the end which is also a duty.

Virtue, being a coincidence of the rational will, with every duty firmly settled in the character, is, like everything formal, only one and the same. But, as regards the end of actions, which is also duty, that is, as regards the matter which one ought to make an end, there may be several virtues; and as the obligation to its maxim is called a duty of virtue, it follows that there are also several duties of virtue.

The supreme principle of ethics (the doctrine of virtue) is: "Act on a maxim, the ends of which are such as it might be a universal law for everyone to have." On this principle a man is an end to himself as well as others, and it is not enough that he is not permitted to use either himself or others merely as means (which would imply that be might be indifferent to them), but it is in itself a duty of every man to make mankind in general his end.

The principle of ethics being a categorical imperative does not admit of proof, but it admits of a justification from principles of pure practical reason. Whatever in relation to mankind, to oneself, and others, can be an end, that is an end for pure practical reason: for this is a faculty of assigning ends in general; and to be indifferent to them, that is, to take no interest in them, is a contradiction; since in that case it would not determine the maxims of actions (which always involve an end), and consequently would cease to be practical reasons. Pure reason, however, cannot command any ends a priori, except so far as it declares the same to be also a duty, which duty is then called a duty of virtue.

## X. The Supreme Principle of Jurisprudence was Analytical; that of Ethics is Synthetical

That external constraint, so far as it withstands that which hinders the external freedom that agrees with general laws (as an obstacle of the obstacle thereto), can be consistent with ends generally, is clear on the principle of contradiction, and I need not go beyond the notion of freedom in order to see it, let the end which each may be what he will. Accordingly, the supreme principle of jurisprudence is an analytical principle. On the contrary the principle of ethics goes beyond the notion of external freedom and, by general laws, connects further with it an end which it makes a duty. This principle, therefore, is synthetic. The possibility of it is contained in the Deduction (Sec. ix.).

This enlargement of the notion of duty beyond that of external freedom and of its limitation by the merely formal condition of its constant harmony; this, I say, in which, instead of constraint from without, there is set up freedom within, the power of self-constraint, and that not by the help of other inclinations, but by pure practical reason (which scorns all such help), consists in this fact, which raises it above juridical duty; that by it ends are proposed from which jurisprudence altogether abstracts. In the case of the moral imperative, and the supposition of freedom which it necessarily involves, the law, the power (to fulfil it) and the rational will that determines the maxim, constitute all the elements that form the notion of juridical duty. But in the imperative, which commands the duty of virtue, there is added, besides the notion of self-constraint, that of an end; not one that we have, but that we ought to have, which, therefore, pure practical reason has in itself, whose highest, unconditional end (which, however, continues to be duty) consists in this: that virtue is its own end and, by deserving well of men, is also its own reward. Herein it shines so brightly as an ideal to human perceptions, it seems to cast in the shade even holiness itself, which is never tempted to transgression. This, however, is an illusion arising from the fact that as we have no measure for the degree of strength, except the greatness of the obstacles which might have been overcome (which in our case are the inclinations), we are led to mistake the subjective conditions of estimation of a magnitude for the objective conditions of the magnitude itself. But when compared with human ends, all of which have their obstacles to be overcome, it is true that the worth of virtue itself, which is its own end, far outweighs the worth of all the utility and all the empirical ends and advantages which it may have as consequences.

With all his failings, man is still

Better than angels void of will.

We may, indeed, say that man is obliged to virtue (as a moral strength). For although the power (facultas) to overcome all imposing sensible impulses by virtue of his freedom can and must be presupposed, yet this power regarded as strength (robur) is something that must be acquired by the moral spring (the idea of the law) being elevated by contemplation of the dignity of the pure law of reason in us, and at the same time also by exercise.

## XI. According to the preceding Principles, the Scheme of Duties of Virtue may be thus exhibited

The Material Element of the Duty of Virtue

Internal Duty of Virtue External Virtue of Duty

My Own End, The End of Others, which is also my the promotion of

Duty which is also my

Duty

(My own (The Happiness

Perfection) of Others)

The Law which is The End which is also Spring also Spring

On which the On which the

Morality Legality of every free determination of will rests

The Formal Element of the Duty of Virtue.

## XII. Preliminary Notions of the Susceptibility of the Mind for Notions of Duty generally

These are such moral qualities as, when a man does not possess them, he is not bound to acquire them. They are: the moral feeling, conscience, love of one's neighbour, and respect for ourselves (self-esteem). There is no obligation to have these, since they are subjective conditions of susceptibility for the notion of duty, not objective conditions of morality. They are all sensitive and antecedent, but natural capacities of mind (praedispositio) to be affected by notions of duty; capacities which it cannot be regarded as a duty to have, but which every man has, and by virtue of which he can be brought under obligation. The consciousness of them is not of empirical origin, but can only follow on that of a moral law, as an effect of the same on the mind.

## A. THE MORAL FEELING

This is the susceptibility for pleasure or displeasure, merely from the consciousness of the agreement or disagreement of our action with the law of duty. Now, every determination of the elective will proceeds from the idea of the possible action through the feeling of pleasure or displeasure in taking an interest in it or its effect to the deed; and here the sensitive state (the affection of the internal sense) is either a pathological or a moral feeling. The former is the feeling that precedes the idea of the law, the latter that which may follow it.

Now it cannot be a duty to have a moral feeling, or to acquire it; for all consciousness of obligation supposes this feeling in order that one may become conscious of the necessitation that lies in the notion of duty; but every man (as a moral being) has it originally in himself; the obligation, then, can only extend to the cultivation of it and the strengthening of it even by admiration of its inscrutable origin; and this is effected by showing how it is just, by the mere conception of reason, that it is excited most strongly, in its own purity and apart from every pathological stimulus; and it is improper to call this feeling a moral sense; for the word sense generally means a theoretical power of perception directed to an object; whereas the moral feeling (like pleasure and displeasure in general) is something merely subjective, which supplies no knowledge. No man is wholly destitute of moral feeling, for if he were totally unsusceptible of this sensation he would be morally dead; and, to speak in the language of physicians, if the moral vital force could no longer produce any effect on this feeling, then his humanity would be dissolved (as it were by chemical laws) into mere animality and be irrevocably confounded with the mass of other physical beings. But we have no special sense for (moral) good and evil any more than for truth, although such expressions are often used; but we have a susceptibility of the free elective will for being moved by pure practical reason and its law; and it is this that we call the moral feeling.

## B. OF CONSCIENCE

Similarly, conscience is not a thing to be acquired, and it is not a duty to acquire it; but every man, as a moral being, has it originally within him. To be bound to have a conscience would be as much as to say to be under a duty to recognize duties. For conscience is practical reason which, in every case of law, holds before a man his duty for acquittal or condemnation; consequently it does not refer to an object, but only to the subject (affecting the moral feeling by its own act); so that it is an inevitable fact, not an obligation and duty. When, therefore, it is said, "This man has no conscience," what is meant is that he pays no heed to its dictates. For if he really had none, he would not take credit to himself for anything done according to duty, nor reproach himself with violation of duty, and therefore he would be unable even to conceive the duty of having a conscience.

I pass by the manifold subdivisions of conscience, and only observe what follows from what has just been said, namely, that there is no such thing as an erring conscience. No doubt it is possible sometimes to err in the objective judgement whether something is a duty or not; but I cannot err in the subjective whether I have compared it with my practical (here judicially acting) reason for the purpose of that judgement: for if I erred I would not have exercised practical judgement at all, and in that case there is neither truth nor error. Unconscientiousness is not want of conscience, but the propensity not to heed its judgement. But when a man is conscious of having acted according to his conscience, then, as far as regards guilt or innocence, nothing more can be required of him, only he is bound to enlighten his understanding as to what is duty or not; but when it comes or has come to action, then conscience speaks involuntarily and inevitably. To act conscientiously can, therefore, not be a duty, since otherwise it would be necessary to have a second conscience, in order to be conscious of the act of the first.

The duty here is only to cultivate our conscience, to quicken our attention to the voice of the internal judge, and to use all means to secure obedience to it, and is thus our indirect duty.

## C. OF LOVE TO MEN

Love is a matter of feeling, not of will or volition, and I cannot love because I will to do so, still less because I ought (I cannot be necessitated to love); hence there is no such thing as a duty to love. Benevolence, however (amor benevolentiae), as a mode of action, may be subject to a law of duty. Disinterested benevolence is often called (though very improperly) love; even where the happiness of the other is not concerned, but the complete and free surrender of all one's own ends to the ends of another (even a superhuman) being, love is spoken of as being also our duty. But all duty is necessitation or constraint, although it may be self-constraint according to a law. But what is done from constraint is not done from love.

It is a duty to do good to other men according to our power, whether we love them or not, and this duty loses nothing of its weight, although we must make the sad remark that our species, alas! is not such as to be found particularly worthy of love when we know it more closely. Hatred of men, however, is always hateful: even though without any active hostility it consists only in complete aversion from mankind (the solitary misanthropy). For benevolence still remains a duty even towards the manhater, whom one cannot love, but to whom we can show kindness.

To hate vice in men is neither duty nor against duty, but a mere feeling of horror of vice, the will having no influence on the feeling nor the feeling on the will. Beneficence is a duty. He who often practises this, and sees his beneficent purpose succeed, comes at last really to love him whom he has benefited. When, therefore, it is said: "Thou shalt love thy neighbour as thyself," this does not mean, "Thou shalt first of all love, and by means of this love (in the next place) do him good"; but: "Do good to thy neighbour, and this beneficence will produce in thee the love of men (as a settled habit of inclination to beneficence)."

The love of complacency (amor complacentiae,) would therefore alone be direct. This is a pleasure immediately connected with the idea of the existence of an object, and to have a duty to this, that is, to be necessitated to find pleasure in a thing, is a contradiction.

## D. OF RESPECT

Respect (reverentia) is likewise something merely subjective; a feeling of a peculiar kind not a judgement about an object which it would be a duty to effect or to advance. For if considered as duty it could only be conceived as such by means of the respect which we have for it. To have a duty to this, therefore, would be as much as to say to be bound in duty to have a duty. When, therefore, it is said: "Man has a duty of self-esteem," this is improperly stated, and we ought rather to say: "The law within him inevitably forces from him respect for his own being, and this feeling (which is of a peculiar kind) is a basis of certain duties, that is, of certain actions which may be consistent with his duty to himself." But we cannot say that he has a duty of respect for himself; for he must have respect for the law within himself, in order to be able to conceive duty at all.

### XIII. General Principles of the Metaphysics of Morals in the treatment of Pure Ethics

First. A duty can have only a single ground of obligation; and if two or more proof of it are adduced, this is a certain mark that either no valid proof has yet been given, or that there are several distinct duties which have been regarded as one.

For all moral proofs, being philosophical, can only be drawn by means of rational knowledge from concepts, not like mathematics, through the construction of concepts. The latter science admits a variety of proofs of one and the same theorem; because in intuition a priori there may be several properties of an object, all of which lead back to the very same principle. If, for instance, to prove the duty of veracity, an argument is drawn first from the harm that a lie causes to other men; another from the worthlessness of a liar and the violation of his own self-respect, what is proved in the former argument is a duty of benevolence, not of veracity, that is to say, not the duty which required to be proved, but a different one. Now, if, in giving a variety of proof for one and the same theorem, we flatter ourselves that the multitude of reasons will compensate the lack of weight in each taken separately, this is a very unphilosophical resource, since it betrays trickery and dishonesty; for several insufficient proofs placed beside one another do not produce certainty, nor even probability. They should advance as reason and consequence in a series, up to the sufficient reason, and it is only in this way that they can have the force of proof. Yet the former is the usual device of the rhetorician.

Secondly. The difference between virtue and vice cannot be sought in the degree in which certain maxims are followed, but only in the specific quality of the maxims (their relation to the law). In other words, the vaunted principle of Aristotle, that virtue is the mean between two vices, is false.  For instance, suppose that good management is given as the mean between two vices, prodigality and avarice; then its origin as a virtue can neither be defined as the gradual diminution of the former vice (by saving), nor as the increase of the expenses of the miserly. These vices, in fact, cannot be viewed as if they, proceeding as it were in opposite directions, met together in good management; but each of them has its own maxim, which necessarily contradicts that of the other.

For the same reason, no vice can be defined as an excess in the practice of certain actions beyond what is proper (e.g., Prodigalitas est excessus in consumendis opibus); or, as a less exercise of them than is fitting (Avaritia est defectus, etc.). For since in this way the degree is left quite undefined, and the question whether conduct accords with duty or not, turns wholly on this, such an account is of no use as a definition.

Thirdly. Ethical virtue must not be estimated by the power we attribute to man of fulfilling the law; but, conversely, the moral power must be estimated by the law, which commands categorically; not, therefore, by the empirical knowledge that we have of men as they are, but by the rational knowledge how, according to the ideas of humanity, they ought to be. These three maxims of the scientific treatment of ethics are opposed to the older apophthegms:

1. There is only one virtue and only one vice.

2. Virtue is the observance of the mean path between two opposite vices.

3. Virtue (like prudence) must be learned from experience.

## XIV. Of Virtue in General

Virtue signifies a moral strength of will. But this does not exhaust the notion; for such strength might also belong to a holy (superhuman) being, in whom no opposing impulse counteracts the law of his rational will; who therefore willingly does everything in accordance with the law. Virtue then is the moral strength of a man's will in his obedience to duty; and this is a moral necessitation by his own law giving reason, inasmuch as this constitutes itself a power executing the law. It is not itself a duty, nor is it a duty to possess it (otherwise we should be in duty bound to have a duty), but it commands, and accompanies its command with a moral constraint (one possible by laws of internal freedom). But since this should be irresistible, strength is requisite, and the degree of this strength can be estimated only by the magnitude of the hindrances which man creates for himself, by his inclinations. Vices, the brood of unlawful dispositions, are the monsters that he has to combat; wherefore this moral strength as fortitude (fortitudo moralis) constitutes the greatest and only true martial glory of man; it is also called the true wisdom, namely, the practical, because it makes the ultimate end of the existence of man on earth its own end. Its possession alone makes man free, healthy, rich, a king, etc., nor either chance or fate deprive him of this, since he possesses himself, and the virtuous cannot lose his virtue.

All the encomiums bestowed on the ideal of humanity in its moral perfection can lose nothing of their practical reality by the examples of what men now are, have been, or will probably be hereafter; anthropology which proceeds from mere empirical knowledge cannot impair anthroponomy which is erected by the unconditionally legislating reason; and although virtue may now and then be called meritorious (in relation to men, not to the law), and be worthy of reward, yet in itself, as it is its own end, so also it must be regarded as its own reward.

Virtue considered in its complete perfection is, therefore, regarded not as if man possessed virtue, but as if virtue possessed the man, since in the former case it would appear as though he had still had the choice (for which he would then require another virtue, in order to select virtue from all other wares offered to him). To conceive a plurality of virtues (as we unavoidably must) is nothing else but to conceive various moral objects to which the (rational) will is led by the single principle of virtue; and it is the same with the opposite vices. The expression which personifies both is a contrivance for affecting the sensibility, pointing, however, to a moral sense. Hence it follows that an aesthetic of morals is not a part, but a subjective exposition of the Metaphysic of Morals; in which the emotions that accompany the force of the moral law make the that force to be felt; for example: disgust, horror, etc., which gives a sensible moral aversion in order to gain the precedence from the merely sensible incitement.

## XV. Of the Principle on which Ethics is separated from

## Jurisprudence

This separation on which the subdivision of moral philosophy in general rests, is founded on this: that the notion of freedom, which is common to both, makes it necessary to divide duties into those of external and those of internal freedom; the latter of which alone are ethical. Hence this internal freedom which is the condition of all ethical duty must be discussed as a preliminary (discursus praeliminaris), just as above the doctrine of conscience was discussed as the condition of all duty.

## REMARKS

Of the Doctrine of Virtue on the Principle Of Internal Freedom.

Habit (habitus) is a facility of action and a subjective perfection of the elective will. But not every such facility is a free habit (habitus libertatis); for if it is custom (assuetudo), that is, a uniformity of action which, by frequent repetition, has become a necessity, then it is not a habit proceeding from freedom, and therefore not a moral habit. Virtue therefore cannot be defined as a habit of free law-abiding actions, unless indeed we add "determining itself in its action by the idea of the law"; and then this habit is not a property of the elective will, but of the rational will, which is a faculty that in adopting a rule also declares it to be a universal law, and it is only such a habit that can be reckoned as virtue. Two things are required for internal freedom: to be master of oneself in a given case (animus sui compos) and to have command over oneself (imperium in semetipsum), that is to subdue his emotions and to govern his passions. With these conditions, the character (indoles) is noble (erecta); in the opposite case, it is ignoble (indoles abjecta serva).

XVI. Virtue requires, first of all, Command over Oneself

Emotions and passions are essentially distinct; the former belong to feeling in so far as this coming before reflection makes it more difficult or even impossible. Hence emotion is called hasty (animus praeceps). And reason declares through the notion of virtue that a man should collect himself; but this weakness in the life of one's understanding, joined with the strength of a mental excitement, is only a lack of virtue (Untugend), and as it were a weak and childish thing, which may very well consist with the best will, and has further this one good thing in it, that this storm soon subsides. A propensity to emotion (e.g., resentment) is therefore not so closely related to vice as passion is. Passion, on the other hand, is the sensible appetite grown into a permanent inclination (e. g., hatred in contrast to resentment). The calmness with which one indulges it leaves room for reflection and allows the mind to frame principles thereon for itself; and thus when the inclination falls upon what contradicts the law, to brood on it, to allow it to root itself deeply, and thereby to take up evil (as of set purpose) into one's maxim; and this is then specifically evil, that is, it is a true vice.

Virtue, therefore, in so far as it is based on internal freedom, contains a positive command for man, namely, that he should bring all his powers and inclinations under his rule (that of reason); and this is a positive precept of command over himself which is additional to the prohibition, namely, that he should not allow himself to be governed by his feelings and inclinations (the duty of apathy); since, unless reason takes the reins of government into its own hands, the feelings and inclinations play the master over the man.

## XVII. Virtue necessarily presupposes Apathy (considered as Strength)

This word (apathy) has come into bad repute, just as if it meant want of feeling, and therefore subjective indifference with respect to the objects of the elective will; it is supposed to be a weakness. This misconception may be avoided by giving the name moral apathy to that want of emotion which is to be distinguished from indifference. In the former, the feelings arising from sensible impressions lose their influence on the moral feeling only because the respect for the law is more powerful than all of them together. It is only the apparent strength of a fever patient that makes even the lively sympathy with good rise to an emotion, or rather degenerate into it. Such an emotion is called enthusiasm, and it is with reference to this that we are to explain the moderation which is usually recommended in virtuous practices:

Insani sapiens nomen ferat, aequus uniqui

Ultra quam satis est virtutem si petat ipsam.

For otherwise it is absurd to imagine that one could be too wise or too virtuous. The emotion always belongs to the sensibility, no matter by what sort of object it may be excited. The true strength of virtue is the mind at rest, with a firm, deliberate resolution to bring its law into practice. That is the state of health in the moral life; on the contrary, the emotion, even when it is excited by the idea of the good, is a momentary glitter which leaves exhaustion after it. We may apply the term fantastically virtuous to the man who will admit nothing to be indifferent in respect of morality (adiaphora), and who strews all his steps with duties, as with traps, and will not allow it to be indifferent whether a man eats fish or flesh, drink beer or wine, when both agree with him; a micrology which, if adopted into the doctrine of virtue, would make its rule a tyranny.

## REMARK

Virtue is always in progress, and yet always begins from the beginning. The former follows from the fact that, objectively considered, it is an ideal and unattainable, and yet it is a duty constantly to approximate to it. The second is founded subjectively on the nature of man which is affected by inclinations, under the influence of which virtue, with its maxims adopted once for all, can never settle in a position of rest; but, if it is not rising, inevitably falls; because moral maxims cannot, like technical, be based on custom (for this belongs to the physical character of the determination of will); but even if the practice of them become a custom, the agent would thereby lose the freedom in the choice of his maxims, which freedom is the character of an action done from duty.

## ON_CONSCIENCE

The consciousness of an internal tribunal in man (before which "his thoughts accuse or excuse one another") is CONSCIENCE.

Every man has a conscience, and finds himself observed by an inward judge which threatens and keeps him in awe (reverence combined with fear); and this power which watches over the laws within him is not something which he himself (arbitrarily) makes, but it is incorporated in his being. It follows him like his shadow, when he thinks to escape. He may indeed stupefy himself with pleasures and distractions, but cannot avoid now and then coming to himself or awaking, and then he at once perceives its awful voice. In his utmost depravity, he may, indeed, pay no attention to it, but he cannot avoid hearing it.

Now this original intellectual and (as a conception of duty) moral capacity, called conscience, has this peculiarity in it, that although its business is a business of man with himself, yet he finds himself compelled by his reason to transact it as if at the command of another person. For the transaction here is the conduct of a trial (causa) before a tribunal. But that he who is accused by his conscience should be conceived as one and the same person with the judge is an absurd conception of a judicial court; for then the complainant would always lose his case. Therefore, in all duties the conscience of the man must regard another than himself as the judge of his actions, if it is to avoid self-contradiction. Now this other may be an actual or a merely ideal person which reason frames to itself. Such an idealized person (the authorized judge of conscience) must be one who knows the heart; for the tribunal is set up in the inward part of man; at the same time he must also be all-obliging, that is, must be or be conceived as a person in respect of whom all duties are to be regarded as his commands; since conscience is the inward judge of all free actions. Now, since such a moral being must at the same time possess all power (in heaven and earth), since otherwise he could not give his commands their proper effect (which the office of judge necessarily requires), and since such a moral being possessing power over all is called GOD, hence conscience must be conceived as the subjective principle of a responsibility for one's deeds before God; nay, this latter concept is contained (though it be only obscurely) in every moral self-consciousness.

*THE END*